HISTORY OF SPORTS

# THE HISTORY OF FOOTBALL

by Brendan Flynn

pogo

## Ideas for Parents and Teachers

Pogo Books let children practice reading informational text while introducing them to nonfiction features such as headings, labels, sidebars, maps, and diagrams, as well as a table of contents, glossary, and index.

Carefully leveled text with a strong photo match offers early fluent readers the support they need to succeed.

### Before Reading

- "Walk" through the book and point out the various nonfiction features. Ask the student what purpose each feature serves.
- Look at the glossary together. Read and discuss the words.

### Read the Book

- Have the child read the book independently.
- Invite him or her to list questions that arise from reading.

### After Reading

- Discuss the child's questions. Talk about how he or she might find answers to those questions.
- Prompt the child to think more. Ask: What did you find most surprising about the history of football? Why?

Pogo Books are published by Jump!
5357 Penn Avenue South
Minneapolis, MN 55419
www.jumplibrary.com



Library of Congress Cataloging-in-Publication Data

Names: Flynn, Brendan, 1968- author.
Title: The history of football / By Brendan Flynn.
Description: Minneapolis, MN: Jump!, Inc., [2025]
Series: History of sports | Includes index.
Audience: Ages 7-10
Identifiers: LCCN 2023057276 (print)
LCCN 2023057277 (ebook)
ISBN 9798892130776 (hardcover)
ISBN 9798892130783 (paperback)
ISBN 9798892130790 (ebook)
Subjects: LCSH: Football–History–Juvenile literature.
National Football League–History–Juvenile literature.
Super Bowl–History–Juvenile literature.
Classification: LCC GV950.7 F59175 2025 (print)
LCC GV950.7 (ebook)
DDC 796.332–dc23/eng/20231213
LC record available at https://lccn.loc.gov/2023057276
LC ebook record available at https://lccn.loc.gov/2023057277

Editor: Alyssa Sorenson
Designer: Molly Ballanger

Photo Credits: ATU Studio/Shutterstock, cover (left); Everett Collection/Shutterstock, cover (right), 11 (left); AdShooter/iStock, 1; Mike Flippo/Shutterstock, 3; Timothy T Ludwig/Getty, 4; Sarah Stier/Getty, 5; Lawrence Weslowski Jr/Dreamstime, 6-7; Hum Images/Alamy, 8; Gordon Parks/Library of Congress, 9; Library of Congress, 10-11; OSTILL is Franck Camhi/Shutterstock, 11 (right); AP Images, 12-13; Rich Clarkson/NCAA Photos/Getty, 14-15; lev radin/Shutterstock, 16; Everett Collection/SuperStock, 16-17tl; Focus on Sport/Getty, 16-17tr; Steve Jacobson/Shutterstock, 16-17bl; Bettmann/Getty, 16-17br; Scott Taetsch/Getty, 18; Robin Alam/Icon Sportswire/Getty, 19 (top); Jorge Lemus/NurPhoto/Getty, 19 (bottom); Darryl Webb/AP Images, 20-21; Jason Sponseller/Shutterstock, 23.

Printed in the United States of America at Corporate Graphics in North Mankato, Minnesota.

# TABLE OF CONTENTS

# CHAPTER 1

# TOUCHDOWN!

It is Monday night. Two National Football League (NFL) teams are facing off. The Steelers are playing the Bills. Josh Allen is the **quarterback** for the Bills. He throws the ball.

A **tight end** is open. He catches the ball in the end zone. It's a **touchdown**!

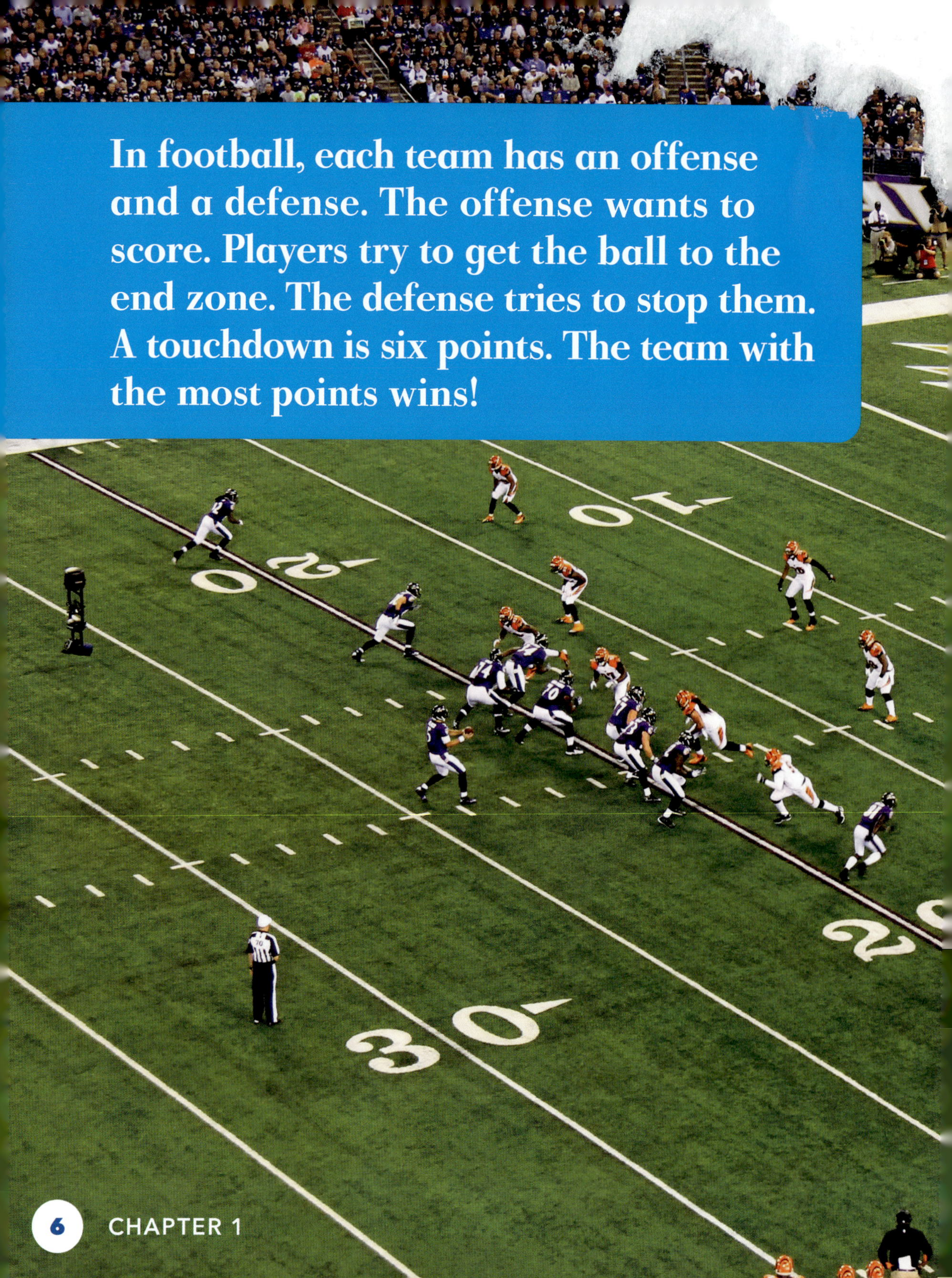

In football, each team has an offense and a defense. The offense wants to score. Players try to get the ball to the end zone. The defense tries to stop them. A touchdown is six points. The team with the most points wins!

# TAKE A LOOK!

What are the areas of a football field? Take a look!

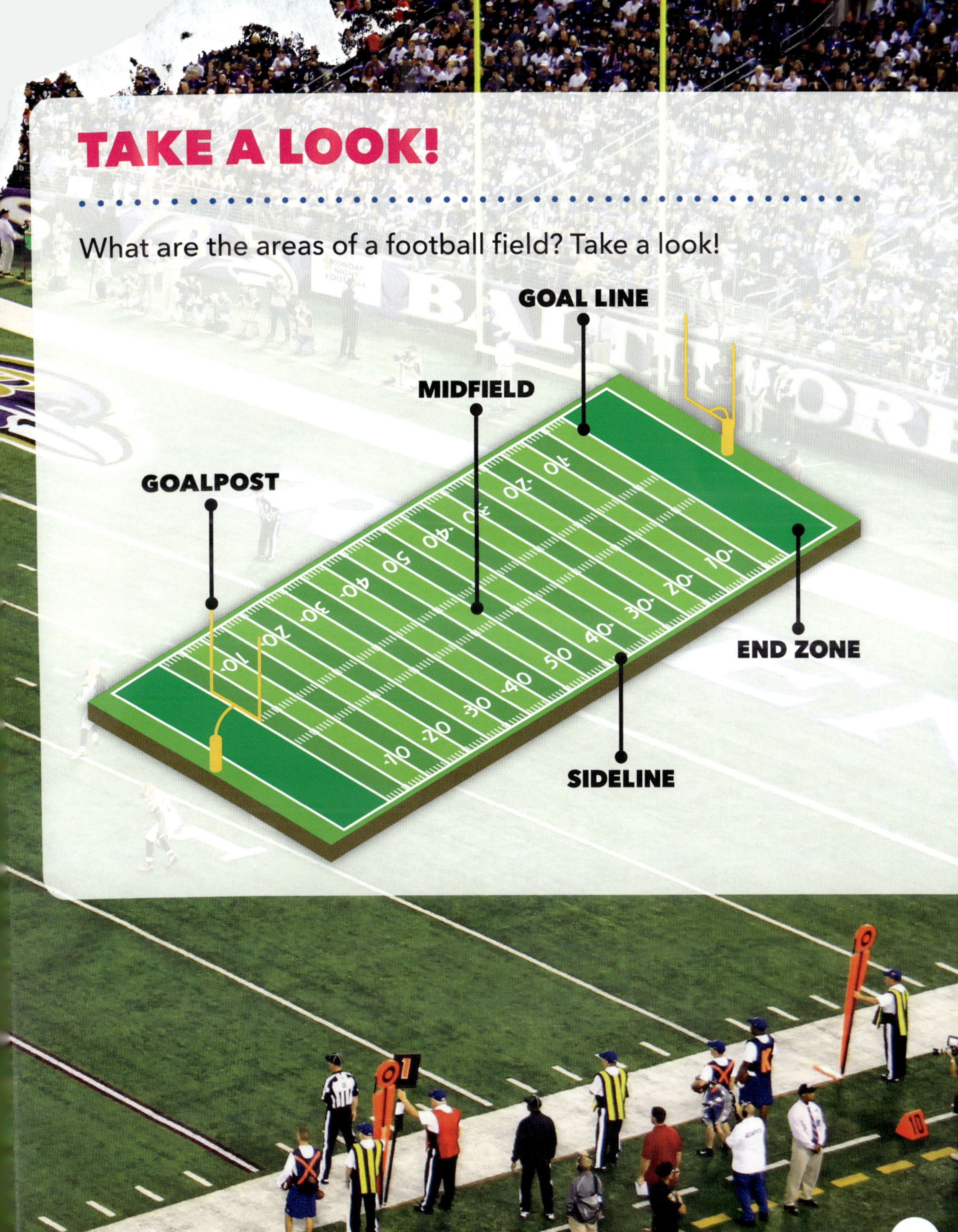

# CHAPTER 2

# FOOTBALL'S HISTORY

Football has been played since the late 1800s. U.S. college students started it. Football is a **contact sport**. Players **tackle**. They often get hurt.

The NFL started in 1920. At first, players wore leather helmets. These were not safe. Players started wearing plastic helmets in the 1940s. Helmets are now made with stronger plastic. They have more padding. This helps prevent **concussions**.

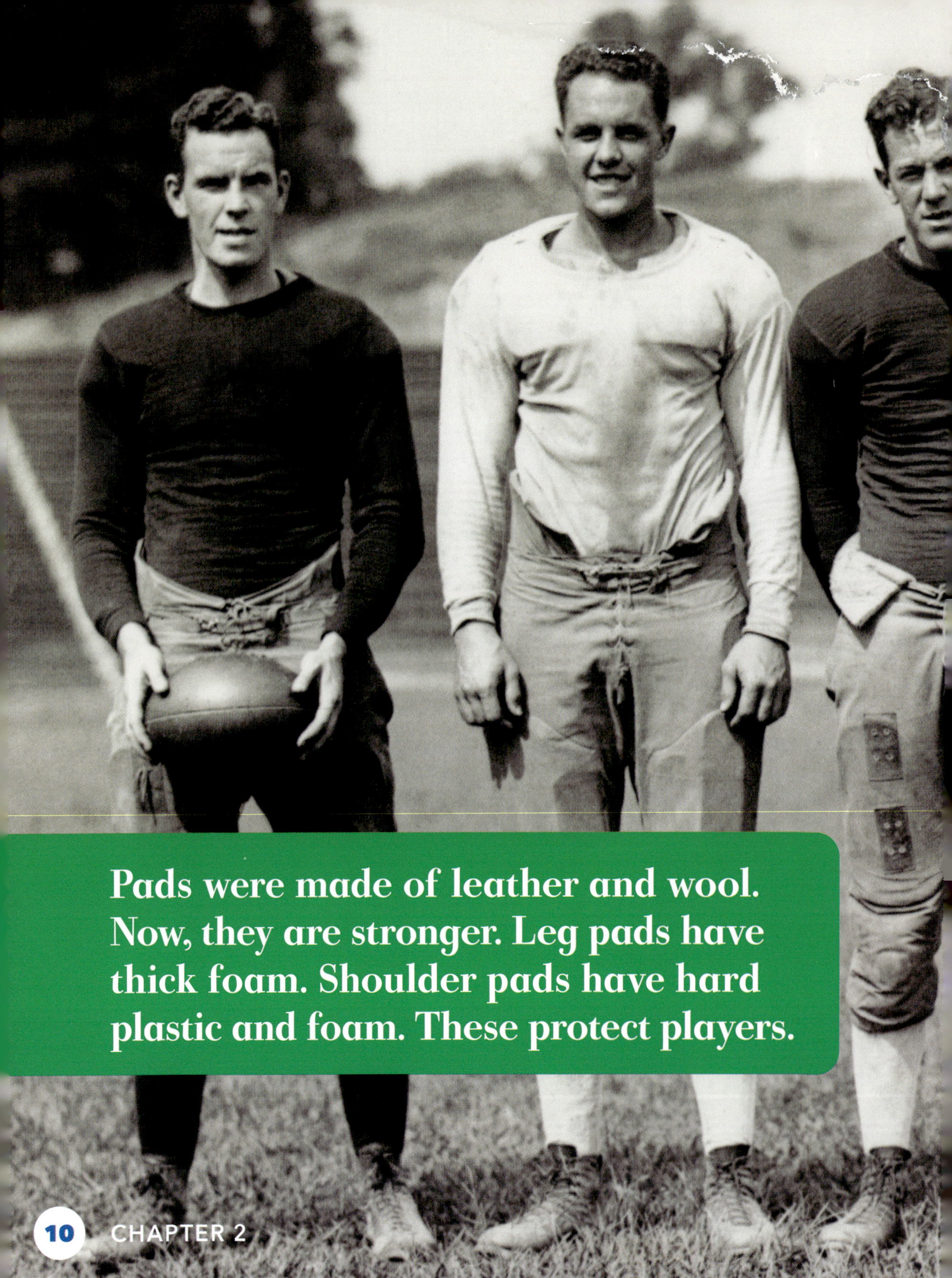

Pads were made of leather and wool. Now, they are stronger. Leg pads have thick foam. Shoulder pads have hard plastic and foam. These protect players.

## TAKE A LOOK!

How have football uniforms changed over time? Take a look!

In the early days, NFL teams did not let Black people play. That changed in 1946. That year, Kenny Washington and Woody Strode joined the Los Angeles Rams. Some teams did not **integrate** until the 1960s. Now, many Black athletes play in the NFL.

## WHAT DO YOU THINK?

As of 2023, no women played in the NFL. Some worked as **officials** and coaches. Do you think women should play in the NFL? Why or why not?

Kenny
Washington
Woody
Strode

1967 Super Bowl

The Super Bowl is the NFL's biggest game. The two best teams play each other. It started in 1967. Tickets to the first Super Bowl were only $12. Today, it is hard to get tickets. They cost thousands of dollars.

## WHAT DO YOU THINK?

The Super Bowl **halftime** show is popular. It used to have marching bands. Now, music stars perform. Why do you think it changed?

Football has had amazing players and coaches. Red Grange was one of the NFL's first stars. **Fans** enjoyed watching him run down the field. Jim Brown used his strength and speed. He broke records. Tom Brady won seven Super Bowls.

Vince Lombardi coached the Green Bay Packers. He helped them win the first two Super Bowls. Now, Super Bowl winners get the Vince Lombardi Trophy.

Vince Lombardi Trophy

Red Grange

Jim Brown

Tom Brady

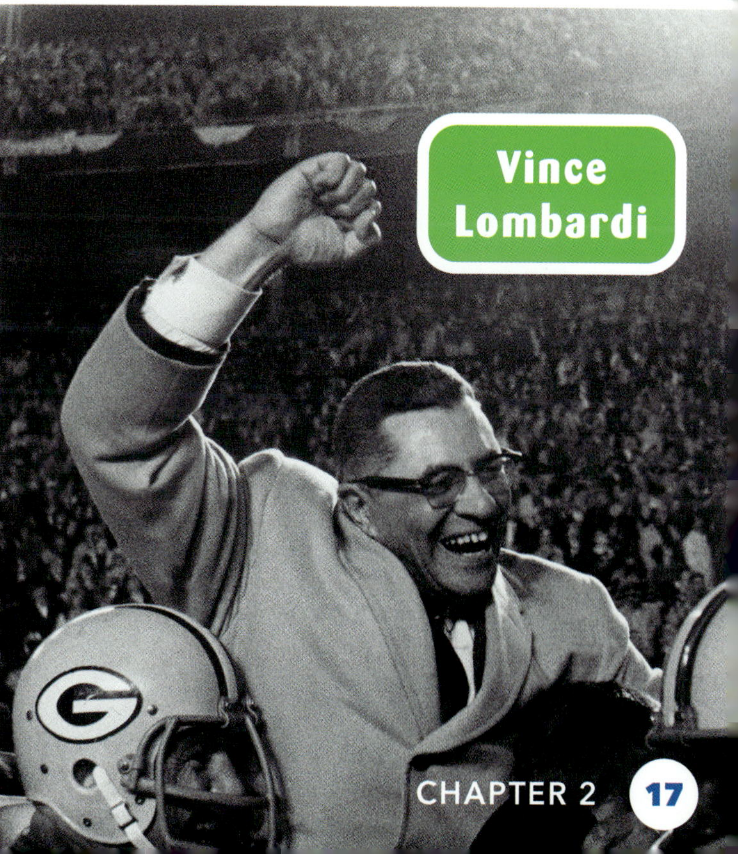
Vince Lombardi

# CHAPTER 3

# FOOTBALL TODAY

**Technology** plays a big role in the NFL today. In the past, officials often missed things that happened during games. Now, they can watch instant replays. They make better calls.

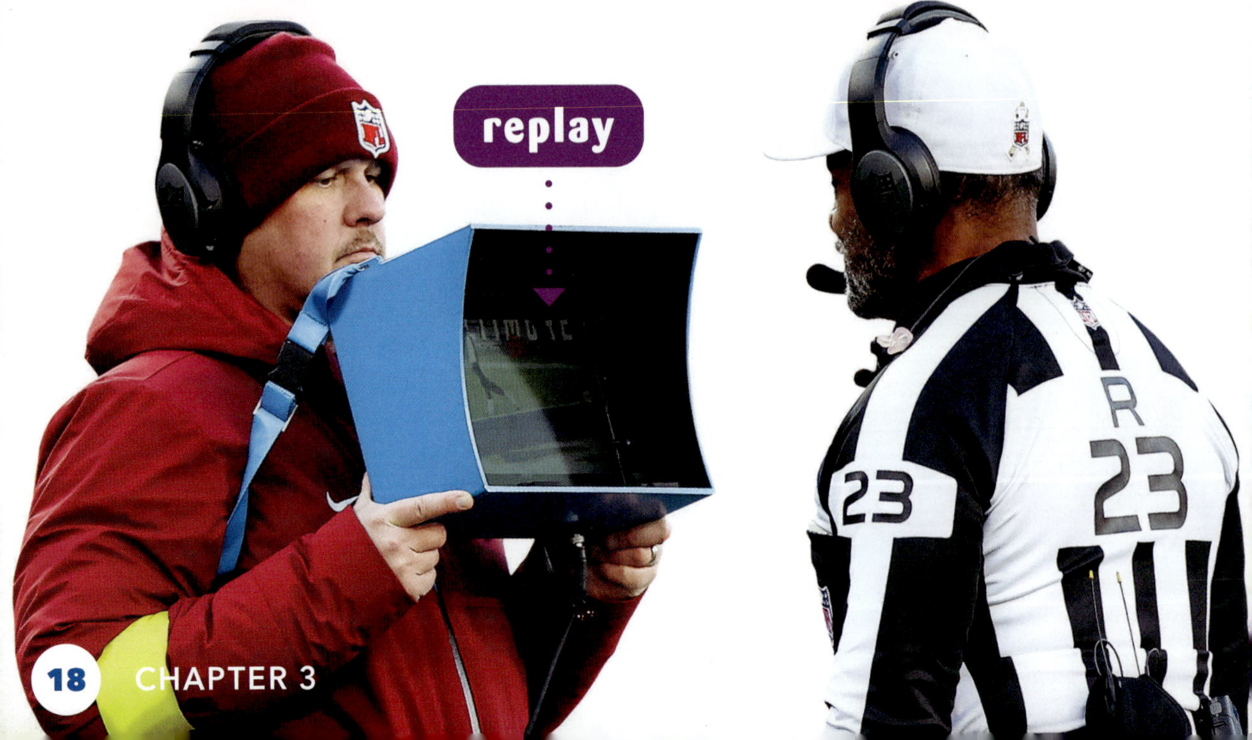

In the past, quarterbacks made their own decisions on the field. Now, they have speakers in their helmets. Coaches talk to them.

MAHOMES
15

Fans cheer for the biggest stars. Patrick Mahomes is a quarterback. He has a strong arm. He has quick feet. Justin Jefferson is a wide receiver. He catches almost anything thrown his way.

Football has changed a lot. But the game is still about teamwork and having fun!

## DID YOU KNOW?

Other forms of football have become popular. Flag football is safer to play. There is no tackling. Arena football is played indoors on small fields. Fans love the action and speed.

# QUICK FACTS & TOOLS

## TIMELINE

**What are the biggest moments in football's history? Take a look!**

**NOVEMBER 6, 1869**
Princeton and Rutgers play the first college football game.

**1876**
A standard set of football rules is created.

**1920**
The American Professional Football Conference forms. Two years later, it changes its name to the National Football League.

**1947**
The Los Angeles Rams become the first team with a logo on their helmets.

**1967**
The Green Bay Packers beat the Kansas City Chiefs in the first Super Bowl.

**1969**
The New York Jets beat the Baltimore Colts 16-7 in Super Bowl III. It is one of the biggest surprise wins in NFL history.

**2021**
Tom Brady wins his seventh Super Bowl. That is more than any other player!

## GLOSSARY

**concussions:** Injuries to the brain caused by hits to the head.

**contact sport:** A sport in which players often run into each other.

**fans:** People who enjoy watching or following sports.

**halftime:** A short break in the middle of a game.

**integrate:** To include people of all races.

**officials:** People who enforce rules during a game.

**quarterback:** The leader of the offense who hands or passes the football to teammates.

**tackle:** To knock or throw a player to the ground to stop them from moving forward.

**technology:** Electronic equipment that helps people do their jobs.

**tight end:** A player who catches passes and makes blocks.

**touchdown:** When a player gets to an opponent's end zone with the football.

# INDEX



# TO LEARN MORE

Finding more information is as easy as 1, 2, 3.

1. Go to www.factsurfer.com
2. Enter "thehistoryoffootball" into the search box.
3. Choose your book to see a list of websites.